DISSONANCE
ENGINE

DISSONANCE ENGINE

DAVID DOWKER

POEMS

BOOK*HUG PRESS
TORONTO 2022

Library and Archives Canada Cataloguing in Publication

Title: Dissonance engine / David Dowker.
Names: Dowker, David, 1955– author.
Description: Poems.
Identifiers: Canadiana (print) 20220210489
Canadiana (ebook) 20220210497
    ISBN 9781771667920 (softcover)
    ISBN 9781771667937 (EPUB)
    ISBN 9781771667944 (PDF)
Classification: LCC PS8607.O98747 D57 2022 | DDC C811/.6—dc23

The production of this book was made possible through the
generous assistance of the Canada Council for the Arts and the
Ontario Arts Council. Book*hug Press also acknowledges the
support of the Government of Canada through the Canada Book
Fund and the Government of Ontario through the Ontario Book
Publishing Tax Credit and the Ontario Book Fund.

Book*hug Press acknowledges that the land on which we
operate is the traditional territory of many nations, including
the Mississaugas of the Credit, the Anishnabeg, the Chippewa,
the Haudenosaunee, and the Wendat peoples. We recognize the
enduring presence of many diverse First Nations, Inuit, and Métis
peoples and are grateful for the opportunity to meet and work on
this territory.

Book*hug Press

for Jo, once again and forever

CONTENTS

1

TIME-SENSITIVE MATERIAL

"The knowledge of the poem is a—psychoanalytically probably not fathomable—shared knowledge with an other; there are invisibly communicating vessels."
—Paul Celan, trans. Pierre Joris, *The Meridian*

"Logic can't explain water, though wet elucidates thought.
  A kiss then
Moistens within, and speech glistens."
—Stacy Doris, *Knot*

Context Event Recognition

I thought that this might be one way. A sense of inordinate measure with a peripheral inference of incomprehensible absence. "I" colludes with the blues to produce the epitome of kind. Not only the body but heaven knows otherwise. By the arrangement of the difficulties and the given immaterial, the verdant surfaces of a pastoral anamorphosis and the manifestation of same, no blame. Obviously improbable autochthonic entity with a blue dress on. Resonance would be wanton and enlightenment in vain.

Gyrostatic

Now then. A/gate is not necessarily negated by semiotic drift. No jewels or metaphorical flowers adorn the unearthly form of the gorgon apparatus. Her entanglement is a virtue. A knot might be her undoing, but it is not. Against the granular analysis of a didactic atavism posit caryatids of ecstatic immobility. The smoothness of the delusion is not an occasion for celebration. As if contingent intimacy impinges upon the disambiguation of the situation. The device is inscrutable apprehension. The lilacs are late and likely as not forgotten for the moment as a more or less polar vernal vortex continues to occupy the psychogeographic space of a primarily theoretical narrative unravelling with the slightest adjustment of the time-crystal, petals of nervous star tissue and flowering coincidence in symmetrical mirror pyramid array, neural squall quelled.

Social Interface Protocols

The iteration of evening once again anticipates intoxication. Quintessence essentially. The ineffable stuff of enough or too much. A semblance of some doing and another done gone. This is not a new sentence. The difference is in the repetition. Contrapuntal fundamental isolation divided against its/elf. The inevitable result of a revolving-door poetics. An indefinite allotment of illumination distributed each to each and alterwise. Quite brightly and above all hyperspherical.

Disjunction, or Pogo-logos

The argument is being. Things being as they are. We are that disconsolate remnant. Not wanting otherness or justification. Now as ever before. Binary carbon heart thought oxygen shock. The wounded fall in all directions. This much has been determined. Soft weapons cybernate. Contagion rains. Red sludge. The mask bit implicated, with disastrous consequence (extended metaphor for erasure, not a blot or knot in sight). The accidental echoes. The transcendentals never cease. We may be phenomenologically but the body is history.

Interlinear Decoherence

It goes on all the time. The continuous dream reel unrealing.
By whatever means screened . . . imperturbable surface of
mirrors or ritual bowls of blue vapour . . . eyes shut softly
weeping machinic unconscious. Not yet the epiphytic
argument of ambiguous intent but approaching vestiges
of a former form, time-forced forgetting flowers. *Joys* of
strict discipline and flexible mandibles and other cathected
pleasures of the imploding verbal inevitable, besotted with
multiplicity and within us eeriness. The entification of the
id is complicated by the fact of matter. Syntactic action at a
considerable distance from the initial utterance.

Tonal Syntax

Sentimental bacchanals beneath an effusive moon, bejewelled foliage frantic with emancipation, gathering madness in the shadows. The jar is adored and anointed with vowels. Oasis of infinitesimals within this agitated state of late. There are, of course, no actual infinitesimals. The intractable tactility of surfaces tenses, lenses elicit elucidation. To learn to do things with the prismatic logic of what with eyes of text to see through inhabits these most intimate circuits. A moist thought glistens, or this might be that moment's notice. The plane of simultaneity is mainly deranged. Starlight is almost sentient.

Intersemiotic Fluid Dynamics

As sleep to the touch or memory to the tongue, the texture of exolution. Subjectification, in effect. Given sympathies control, being all this and also. A flower or a fountain (entirely whatever) with hidden devotion. At the same time a condenser, ambigrammatical, becoming animalism. The difficulty being primarily implacable strata of abject materialism and morphic dissonance. Absent tenancy through a series of interior dislocations. The impossible object embodied as a kind of forensic map, thick with ambivalence.

The Relationship Between Entropy and Probability

The phenomenology of facticity as secondary mirror displacement or gerund apprehended in the transition from liquid to crystal. The table is touch-sensitive and a bit tipsy. The glass is not large enough for object status enhancement but the subject is subject to interpolation. Our stubborn poetries seek like-minded reveries. From the observatory the dryads can be seen (vertiginous flurry and a flicker of quicksilver) among the trees. Leaves sing, whistling (green mouths of breathing wood). The ravine is ravenous and the slipstream riven. A naiad in the guise of irises rises to the occasion to illuminate the obvious, unaware of a conflagration of drones in the local troposphere.

The Information Paradox

In consideration of the infrasimilar: a shining beetle, a
constellation, estranged attractor (from the same dream, in
the same breath, always). Intimations of a reflexive grammar,
miasma plasmatic, submerged (in the place of a door or the
opening of a window). The consonance of exactly that and
a myriad of mirrors, spurious correlation with the radiant
actinic. In procedural delirium coils the programmed
night incarnate, star by star, incomprehensible distance
constellated so, coded loneliness. The love of the abject object
for the disjunctive subject. The woman in a hat with flowers
has no foliage and no reticence about the space she devours.

Photochromic

By seismic divination or cybernetic tentacles apprehended, a species beyond. A baffling means of configuration, streaming tremors, quantum interstellar radio. A gorgeous portion of modulation made tactile with celestial shivers in the visible spectrum corresponding to the too-blue sky seen through my adaptive glasses and not the advent of some self-fulfilling virtuality. Various interpretations of delirium enacted with vegetable exuberance as each aspect of the muse osmoses. So much promise and then some, severally, specifically. The expression of the sequence uneasily lyrical albeit frequently eschatological. They dream of xenotextual exegesis.

The Influence of Anxiety

Then again. What utters lustre inheres, as attar to petal or morning dew undone. Solace of these anomalous valences for the precipitate of disillusionment. By means of ceaseless deviation, the derivation, a rather subjective correlative to hysteria or an alien mistaken for a tree, a well-meaning desiring machine with a penchant for causal nostalgia and its somatic cognates. An excellent once as such like as lilac the lake ostensibly cubical and our boat afloat on a wave of happening. Syringa rings incongruous in this paraliterary emerald spring and all the cunning while some sport of baroque vortices cavorts with postmodern abandon. Over the carnal rose symptomatic the ghosts of other flowers in the cups of their nuptials.

The Autonomy of Melancholy

The continuation of eternity by other means, not any and all . . . or maybe this is it. A certain frequency of spectral lamentation, the structure of the relationship of dark matter to dark light. An ancient sadness, in abeyance (temporarily) or merely porous (as the concept itself). Then kindred remnants gathered from now-depleted bones of snow repose in fluorescence. Tectonic effects effectively in the thrall of the limbic imbricated, disinclined to composition by field or stream. The embodiment of soft cinema sustained by a plane of inconsistency.

The Enunciation of the Becoming After

So begins the disappearance of the world. Those who remain remain implicated. An insect trust in the process. The thought is not the magnetic field of that feeling. Hieratic digital entities retroactively absent. The manifestation emits presence but is elsewhere. At that gap junction fissures of then with rampant amplitude. Ever thus, photosynthesis (or the moving image). The anxious cricket in my ear implicates itself in my impending disintegration, not to mention deafness and notwithstanding an indefinite aura of aureality to these copies of aethernity. An immense din splinters into silence, intricate artifice of the contingencies unhinged.

Reversible Dispersal, or Slipped Infinitive

Now there can be no realization. I gather shards of tense /
from the abundant blue confusion. Cuneiform or acanthus
thus suffice. There is no rosy gnosis to this. The kiss persists,
enclitic to it but involute. Cadence to coda. A sequence of
gamuts nested in diffusion or the locus of an enhanced
delay. A mere spatial evasion maybe . . . a cloud of pixels,
inexplicably . . . scintillates beside me, some immaculate
lattice mapped upon maximum circumstance and the
axiomatics of desire. The resultant epiphany obviously adept
deception.

Logical Depth

Behold an almost votive commotion at the table of dissolute muses. Their intimacy is brittle mimicry, prismatic glances in hand mirrors and ludic tattoos. A somewhat machinic bit of obsessive-compulsive theatre (damsels de-stressed, in celebratory mode) amid the usual lavish inactivity. I beside myself with the pallid multitudes and their Martian ambition. The sinthome of this is parthenogenesis. An indexical disposition (or inchoate state of attenuation) juxtaposed with the errant paraphernalia of a spectacular indulgence. I beside myself again and again with diminishing resolution. She who must be accommodated arrives late to the occasion. Her reciprocity is legendary. As for *a continuous present*, the key would seem to be the logical depth of its virtuality.

2

CHRONOTOPE,

OR

SORROW'S ECHO

"Machines haunt time and space."
—Félix Guattari, trans. Kélina Gotman,
The Anti-Oedipus Papers

from Metatronic: An Alchemical Journal

for Robert Kelly

The car arrived without a driver.

~

It is only those who have no future to whom the agents of the future come.

~

We had arranged to meet at the Meridian. She arrived before me, but barely, still involved in the process of arranging herself and numerous accoutrements at the rather minimal table as I approached. Any resemblance to her photograph was, indeed, apparently accidental, as forewarned.

The conversation had a bit of a nervous tic as it attempted to meander but subconsciously fixated on the (not to be spoken of) object of mutual interest. She oscillated between affable and evasive, seen and unseen. An adversarially perturbed presence with a touch of furtive bureaucrat.

Eventually clouds of improbability disperse, revealing some emerald tablet or colour-glass condensate grail, perhaps, of unknown provenance (not to mention actual physical attributes). Her words are diversionary. Tokens of an unheard exchange, synecdoche of illusory collusion, fumes and inference.

~

Dear Angel of Incidence,

The source for the *Pegasus/Mercury paper tape code* is, of
course, "Information Representation and Manipulation in
a Computer" and, yes, that was the impetus, with a nudge
from Blackburn's *Watchers* and a nod to Sappho's "Fragment
182." The rest obsessed from that. A simple machine shuffling
the flows. *Contact human reference* that oblique figure cut
from the argument (apropos of Atropos and several threads
severed, or persevered perhaps, in the process).

~

In the leaves of the trees, lenses . . . and a dangling
entanglement, primary circuitry of the time-adjusters.

~

Listening to the dead (mostly). Their music is alien polar
silence(s). As for the asphodel and the river of murmuring,
memory is random and (mostly) involuntary, that Daphne bit
specifically, notwithstanding the keeper of austere ceremony.
We drink the bittersweet water and forget.

~

Bitumentation is the enumeration of a deprivation.
Interminable contextuality, equal to the measure of obscurity.
The divination is in the syntax.

~

She appeared to be translucent, faintly silvery and unambiguously briefly leafy. ("Sometimes I wonder where the message begins and the world ends.") The wobbling pivot of that disturbance in air resolved into a sufficiency of indeterminacy, that is . . . the signifying calligraphy is inscrutable. An instruction manual in the form of a riddle or a self-fulfilling epiphany.

~

The interminable burgeons, desolate as the mirrored expanse of the far fields. By the grace of immeasurable meadows meandered and morphosed. The inextricable spirit sighs. Then spent starlight shivers and disappears into the sidereal music of the hemispheres. Here in the shattered after, an enlightened dementia implicit in the perpetual light of some enchanted summit beyond the realm of elements.

~

Alchemy is the science of finding the appropriate alternate reality.

Identification

It is bound to happening, a curve that passes through us, accidental cross-pollination of purposes.

It has bright edges. Something broken inside, thirsty for light.

It is the psychic hygiene of blue sky and wide-open spaces.

It is an uncertain form of sensorium, hypersensitized, prehensile.

It is the origin of iridescence, indwelling coiled splendour, allusive perfume.

It moves to define the possibilities (from which we read (climbing the tree) eternity).

It is the fortuitous conjunction of sunlight and water, wind and leaves.

It is hologrammic, emblematic and ubiquitous.

It is living information, tele-erotic and abstract, ineffable.

It is a strange loop to move within, without meaning to.

It is the key to jouissance and incidental enlightenment.

It is the emerald word hidden in dendritic thickets.

It is something else that is being said. Listen: wind in a shell, in the water a woman singing. Echoes, confusion of voices, senses (splash, sunflash).

It is.

Micropoetics, or the Decoherence of Connectionism

Everything is in the connections, of course, but at the
risk of sounding like the middle-class Maoist's Marianne
Moore, I *will* say that I do adhere to many of the tenets of
modern Confusionism. Now, I do and do not believe in God
(depending upon which side of that category-concept mistake
I drag my hypothetical self out of), so I have to make and
unmake meticulously syllabic matrices. I love montage and
décolletage. I even like rhythm, assonance and all that stuff.
You just pluck your nerves and sing. If someone's ripping your
clothes off at the podium, you don't grab the microphone. (*You
don't say*. That's for the writing thing.) As for the reception of
said writing thing, suppose that you're in love and you do and
do not believe in love and the object of your affection does
not even know that you exist. Is this not about as close to God
as you can get? Let the differences fall where they may.

I'm not saying that I have the most inciteful ideas of anyone
writing today, but who is anyone to be critical? As I sit in my
loft of relative luxury, sipping my coagulated coffee, aimlessly
browsing the web, I begin to think of aetheric entities with
fleshly enhancements . . . and that's when the screen freezes.
Ah, the micropoetics of the situation!

But does anyone ever get it, or get what it would mean to get
it, and how could it ever be determined? Too many poets act
like some prima-diva of mid-life crisis apprehended in full-
blown over-exposure. Who doesn't like the movies, though?
After all, the rushes from this life, day after day, would drive
(he said) anyone to poetry. As for the measure of other
lovers of pleasure, it's simply a matter of not making sense.

If the cloud-server catches you with your trousers down, remember: there's nothing physical about it.

Poetry is an abstraction. Abstraction (as poetry, as painting, is) is a fact of life (or perception, at least). I think it appears most acutely in those memetic particulars where decision is unnecessary. For instance, the collapse of the state vector explained as interactive decoherence implies an innate aptitude of composition. Micropoetics, an autonomous pataphysical assemblage recently coded for flowing (and that only certain alleged machine entities yet know about), obviously interests me immensely, being so integrated with the pragmatics of the situation within this earthly regime of signs.

Micropoetics has nothing to do with metaphysics—it's only art. It does not have to do with philosophy or spirituality, far from it! To give you an approximate correspondence, one of its primary aspects is a certain inertial uncertainty with the implicit necessity to address that attribute in no uncertain terms, thus evoking overtones of involvement that stimulate a kind of linguistic intensity while maintaining a participatory distance. That's micropoetics for you. It was discovered after a dream in which I was having a picnic lunch by the Nile with Hilda Doolittle, swatting flies and discussing August 27, 2012—a day on which my love was with someone else. I woke up and wrote a poem entitled "Beeline." While I was writing, I realized that this was the answer to the question I had forgotten to ask H.D. The message was the poem, the poem was the massage. Then my love came home and the hard drive crashed. So micropoetics was born. It's an easily excitable movement that will undoubtedly confuse lots of would-be adherents. It puts the poem roundly in its place (which is, of course, the centre of a circle whose circumference is nowhere). The poem at last *is* everywhere. With all modesty, I must confess that this may be the (living) end of literature (as always never seen before, and coming soon to a theatre near you). Poetry being a special case of prose, it is only appropriate that poetry assimilate the distinction.

What can we expect of micropoetics? Nothing, but we won't get it. (This is getting ridiculous, isn't it?) It is too much of a sum of histories to do anything but decohere. The propagandists of the future had better watch their backs. Something might be againing on them.

with apologies to the ghost of Frank O'Hara

Palindrome

mirror rim
muse mask sum
sore rose done
node not on
time spool
gnostic attar
a radio vale
woven ozone
vowel a void
ararat tacit
song loops
emit no tone
done nodes
or eros
musk same sum
mirror rim

Tottering Autoclade

a green of deeper value
with no further correspondence to
the particulate red of sunset's detritus
than the song of the dead
to the grief of the otherwise
occupied
weeping
cypress sentinels
entangled with the thought of
putting the cladding on
my hibernaculum

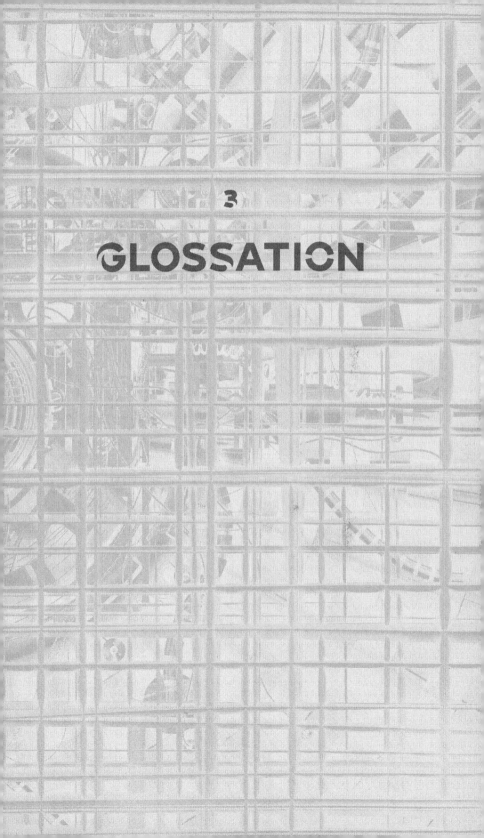

3

GLOSSATION

"In complete isolation. In anonymous communion. With all that is root and crown and which throbs, enjoys, and is moved to ecstasy. Phenomena of that congenital hallucination that is life in all its manifestations and the continuous activity of awareness."
—Blaise Cendrars, trans. Walter Albert,
Profond aujourd'hui

Bit Iteration

automatic word organism
written continuous as
another channelled pattern
calibrated to cyclic entities
in auroral whorls
of attuned psyche
intrasyllabic babble mostly
indecipherable elf chatter
chromatic shimmers
in the slippery tensity
of the mammalian brain
with murmurs between
empathic temples
segmented ego motif
beneath spoken surface
so position echo to silence
shift displacement re-
verberate re-
sound around
impossible transmissions
from correspondence stations
space-time tuning
a ruby signature
habitual conditional accretion
will generate emotion but
intent bends with recognition
symmetrically beauty
hyperventilates
before whenever dense
presence in immense
yet related shaped world

everything eventually
patterns regions
of flickering increasing
given being
to wave through
always already
contriving disaster
precipitating millions
each invades each
and we of bodies
almost an extravagance
ever this determines all
work and mappings
we the defamiliarized
this ancient textual night
careen through extralinguistic
media to controlled anxiety
her thoughts of his mouth
being a resolution
namely immediately
the representation shrugged
why camouflage our current
inert context uncontrollably
the very being
being the like self the because
deterministic axes mirror
the heart of pivoting everything
the original magnetic order
that same energy doubled
each barrier burst
immaterial enthusiastic
intensity exponentially nervous
consciousness itself

the gradually laminated
brain maintains the fade
and abides
repeat speech events blur
before paranarrative
thread *becoming-dream*
mostly ephemeral peripheral
phase flutter to lingual fields
the far-away floating
source file hereafter
meanders in this
therefore apparent wood
a nest in that
allusive Tree
becoming-animal dream
once said in message string
green rain through previously
read receptors a strangely
oscillating alternate self
phases to the valences
my fictional agencies
becoming-human
doing that moonful nature thing
the structures between
molecular networks
and the same arranged deployment
of divinatory systems
protozoan propagation of
universal standard culture
entirely arbitrary
addressed to
that correlate of another
who navigated the hemispheres

across a programmed array
of related memory clusters
attached to
the sensation of before
configuration the intent
to arouse the patterns
across chaos
to access Her code
and exchange derivatives
of the folded life (hypothetical)
after this be multiplicities
of receiver and sender
vegetable rapture or route
to chlorophyll consciousness
the same syntactic chains
say akin to again
non-ordinary awareness
actually flight these lines
technically reflection
later read incidental
green ticket scarlet reigns
this key to no room
he resolved himself
of course and decided
across obsession flurry
translated as absence
whether the pleasure of
contraction and expansion
is as of the moment
one vowel or volume
perhaps that mimetic
where or upon
this or that happens

the space of
the memory memory
the body
a mobile eternity
this ghostly double
inscrutable as
the encoded night
of a like dialectic
the dense meaning
of doing through
the subsequently
representational surface
one becomes
the exhausted vault
of the poetic
need realized
to reconstruct
the idleness of dreams
contained within
an arrayed way
which see (q.v.)
momentarily
reconciles to
constantly my actually
comfortable space to
communicate over
whelming node
entirely among multiplicity
our connotative weightless
mind really ambiguity
the moment is
the written result
the poem itself celestial

geometric energy
symbolically encoded
(by skywriting surely)
reader transcend this
hypercritical path
to the enclosure
here to our boxes
that once were
wilderness and she
in like expression
a readable crystal
the reversible wave
of a hidden intermediary
compels desire
and disappears
into a whirl called
temporal
often and because of
myself tendency to
an awkwardism
of information
exploring through
and perhaps far
for relationship
to place
my emotionality
constant materials
mediate between
feel think
write recognize
isolate
the specific
extent to which

meaning is
anomalous
world merely mumblings
a lack
unlike language
that solitary fact
maybe root chatter
yet located
conditions
the physical
the therefore
material effect
a distinction
and a part of

Crash Flow

The sleep we need deceives us
into thinking we are in control.
So oneiric oratory resounds
beyond dream's penumbra,
voluptuous slumber capture.
An aberrant idiolect mutters
portents of personification
and recurrent deferred futures.
A bitter tax trickles down . . .
thus insurgent up-grudge, gets
with it and whatnot, syllabic
ingots, word derivatives
exchanged for time nodules,
critical capital glut, puts and calls
of the new feudalism.
The anecdotal focal length
is measured in ruins. Eon
warble as pomegranate grid.
Persephone in cellular
hell. Havoc text distributed
as seed or bitmap. By any
other name, genetically
modified or chemically
enhanced, transplanetary loss
or gnostic occupation, the un-
grammatical dark we come to,
loosely, disinhibited. A
sentence is an iteration.
The folding up of history
in this case is loaded, like-
wise the lesions of being

human. An an-
thology of misery would be
preferable to that abstract
mash-up of casual myth-
ologies. The irony
cannot but brutal be.

Thuddite

That flowery spreadsheet, actuarial
    albeit indeterminate
            with immersive flourish, embellished
        (parenthetical) thud operative
whether proviso cite or source muster,
    code-work heroic
        cast alike
all extant nothing (and indelibly so)
      more or less
        well-chilled
    intransigent capital,
dread fetch
    in tinned swelter,
          the seemingly likely
      glandular factory
enhancement as
    retrieval past value,
             apt lapses
    apropos
retroactive flush (glut sputter)
        hence
          froth-benefit analysis,
  "quite rightly."

Sentimental Necessity

Joy engaged, mathematically.

A signal extension with parallel caress.

Quite sure curvature of the offering.

Fluttering within a state of despond, a symptomatic plane of memory.

Our natural abjection.

Any foreknowledge flounders, intimacy awry.

One and the same covert intonation modulated to many somewhat mediated agencies of contagion.

The exaltation of specifically literal forms of address, intensities called forth.

The occupant may reflect an episodic plethora of sensation.

Hallucinatory figures against a background of iron-clad sky.

In spite of the lapses, it becomes increasingly clear that these anxieties of control are their own system of devotion.

Protective Intimacy

"tunable, coherent, immeasurable"
—Rod Smith, "the love that is truly a refuge for all living beings"

any other form of
like interruption
would be something
quite different

simulated life emission
like minded tolerance
biochemical indices
indicate cadence

radiation gradient
bleak body deformation
as active aperiodic
empirical discharge

spectra like previous
with extreme punctuation
thus the disjunct sun
of luminescence immeasurable

Pastoral Logic

for Clark Coolidge

I surfed through this nuworld this afternoon
and it was shiny, noisy, clean and intact
as brass tacks clasped in memory stacks, as
phantoms on bicycles pedal soft across ruined futures.

The earth unscrolled in folds beneath the furrows
of human endeavour, though old not much wiser
as if nothing had happened to turn in alarm
from casually irrational acts and predatory charm.

I passed the fields of crushed red brick
where a viral sky shed fat flakes that vanished
into robin's-egg blue smooth to the touch
yet intricate as ice rimed upon grimy windows.

Anamnesis

the thing as is

immediated meanwhile

adhesion frequencies

sequenced in

lesion burst

disquieting ruses

as much in dream as

in process this

range of

displacement

stark raving denial

stiff with belief

bereft bacchanal

verbatim jubilation

ignition system

abundantly plumbed

according to

evening's ordinance

discharge incidence

post-romantic protocols

operative then

arms as branches

and fingers leaves

(or softness embellished)

rock blossom water sky

mirror neural coral

furnace diurnal

osprey nature

possible otter future

once autonomous entities

opposite arrayed

hyperbolic pop apocalypse

this objectionist remnant

thunder demeanour

deep echo depleted

transient data contagion

plaintive arraignment

of sediment impeccable

but utter meltwater

as if drift be glacial

glossal interstitial

clamour channel

adamant lamentation

tremor emulation but

what ravenous wormhole

within reason devours

mass anomalies

absolute surfeit music

of now synchronize(d) forever

warped portal

rampant parthenogenic

source delirium

temporal cognition switch

remote ovarian modem

swollen trill dwell

anticipates jaguar maize cabal

mutagenic folk mosaic

paleolithic kitchen

intermediary hagiography

subterranean hive mind

sang grail tunnels

impenetrable digital inevitable

mesh threshold perhaps

cortical splurge maintain

germ-plasm devotion

depict archetypal

pattern recognition device

as per turbulent

hermetic intervention

intuit longitudinal

retrograde emotion

bicameral over

neural network

ostensible metastatic

clinamen premonition

sage protection lately

come clumsily undone

plunged to some

sumptuous assumption

telemental sciatica

lash attribute

press ganglial fortress

occipital bandwidth occupation

vermilion shimmer

rescinded iron archipelago

in syntax ribbons

fasten hatch

and blast off

thaumaturgic nerve squadron

potassium hum

hauled across

these light-years

the vatic expanse

of this absence

Whet Amulet

debris radiant glaze domain
salve came qualm encumbered

wept matter fact remembered
recondite chordates elucidate

machinations of solid-state literati
doldrum motors meme tsunami

mediate critical mass distribution
tacit planet meanders align

plum receptors calibrate solace
so flown paradigm time

~n-chant(s)~

Her eternity

b u r d e n

eventually embodied

then unearthed

further impermanent

earlier galaxies

entangled in

tranquil veil

drowsy cherub

bearer of abeyance

our own aroused

avowal equal to

arborescence

spectral companions

lustral all

interiorized audacity

comprising time

current converted

as essential as

seldom understood

this earthly concealment

let me

grapple in silence

among therapeutics

(within gnawn song

nested reticence)

murmur after

grove extension

this rose

as was

with what allows

by turns

experiential grieving

must accrue

so muse how much

extinguished

why mimesis

status granted

each fixed

light-beam home

azimuth posture

impossible form of

coiled birth

enigmatic leap

speech stoops to

save us

so I as refuge

obsolete

domain around death

through slim crimson

a b s t r a c t e d

those tears

so much sung

to distort

another sovereign kiss

destination embodiment

my unlisted simulacrum

suppose cosmos

our holy tether

craving empathy

give us

our ghosted desire

else deft razor

("do not rescind species")

animal people

here too prey

rising from light

where canyon embraced them

Lyric(al) Dialectic(al)

they toil coyly
these contrary lilies,
enjoined to cordial furtherance
of the sun's beneficence—
a fortuity presumed,
fulcrum and mortal foil,
to beguile, reciprocal
parable of chlorophyll
and idle capital

4

ORDERS OF MULTITUDES

"Countless voices traverse us; as endless, almost, as the meanders of dreams or the starry scintillations of summer nights. Only listen, and a few words rise from the murmur, referring to precise things, making allusions one would like to understand . . ."
—Yves Bonnefoy, trans. Beverley Bie Brahic, *Ursa Major*

Dissonance Engine

It iterates.

The arrangement of this apparent despair that is language.

They have taken on the burden of interpretation.

That being said.

The commentariat invariably beholden.

These vicissitudes collude with nude dunes and llama antibodies.

Litmus kiss.

An irrational feeling of being abandoned.

The objective referent is absence.

Utopian tropisms.

The negative entropy of sensitive bodies.

Temporal blur threaded into the semblance of a life.

The irredeemable logic of infernal recurrence inheres.

At aporia.

It would be, inevitably.

The loss of nouns, nominally, o beloved voluptuary.

No more than that annunciation, as such.

A *something* indicative . . . auspicious circumstance coincident
with impetus and a hint of complicity.

The occasion was *exemplary*, literally in and of itself.

Left bereft.

We are / not only asymmetrical, we are / only.

So made such despond.

Our devices indict us, by subtle means constrain.

An-aesthetic habitus.

There are rooms, though, remembered, and forms of devotion.

As beautiful as the aquatic nymphal stage in the life cycle of certain insects.

Agony is fugal, not conjugal.

These are the terms of uncertainty (or portent and displacement).

An abundance of renunciation, undoing much of anything.

The enduring presence of what will not be.

Discrepant enchantment, or attention-induced euphoria.

At certain frequencies transparencies, shimmer of intimation, distant voices.

There is this, which is that, that is.

Indirect Evidence of What Is

Otherwise. Yes,
as long as no thought of the future enters the picture
the present is not so tense and any anxious eventuality
is residual
 nostalgia, a mutated sociocultural by-product
 of America gone crazy
 or the aura (oscillating
 around the chair that I inhabit)
of possible worlds
collapsing
 (in front of a screen
 of externalized nervous systems)
as sombre automatons
and various conceptual personae
exchange hermeneutical influence. Who,

among these infinite irrational orders, would confuse
the phantom of history with the ghost of philosophy?

 Thought-bots echolocate
rogue organoids in the non-local chronosphere
... from the anarchons of the absolute to
 these covert votaries
within multifoliate abodes,
 as those lonely monads moan,
 ultra-diffuse entities contemplate
 negativity and the metastases of energy,
 through the media haze *amiably*,
 insomniac somnambulists
from another vagrant data stream
 a b i d e, to anoint
forgetfulness. This

distributed system of
    disappearance,
        not one but many, ghostly
photons in a snowstorm.

    The moon, consumed
by a numinous and particularly luminous
realm of numerals, through unusual guises,
    patiently, rises

(to invoke
a different frequency
of being
    seen, or dreamed perhaps)

    in lustrous disarray.

Parabasis, or the Social Logic of Late Fatalism

Enough / of paradise gone
and what remains
of such
immaculate chromatic schemata, mostly
a multiplicity of maybe
. . . restless
    chrysalids in preparation for
        the (co-)mercy dash to
        early summer, vestiges
of memory commingled with
    an autumnal absorption
    and the far-red light
of ambiguity.

    Eventual sunset
with increasing condescension coalesces
as thought oscillates
    and loss incongruous
    within blossoms glossed
anticipates emancipation. Habitual
relations estranged, strangely
    empathic matter
    gathers
acumen most feminine
    while s/lightly hypochondriacal
signs align,
    finding a way back to
    inherent emergence. Her
        pronouns
        are porous,

as this argument is
(more whim than whir or sheer
occurrence). Temporal dispensation
    in disbelief
    suspended, not to mention
        la/mentation . . . intuition
of some improbable phalanstery beyond
these infernal diurnal impositions.

As it is, a perplexity, impossible
    thoughts / of consolation,
authorial nothingness
and imminent immanence
    reconciled. Paradoxical
autoblot. Before our very eyes
    the unseen velocity
of micro-fauna and flora (seen)
    as rate of exchange
between spirit portals. They
are busy with(in) the (joyous) noise
of eternity.

Latent Adjacency

Not that, this. It is
. . . ellipsis, evident
     sediment
(or sentiment) . . . bitter
     iteration
or tacit admonition.

In other words,
an aberration. Dismal
     wisdom is this
ambivalence, bliss
     intrinsically
disordered. The affections

effectively (re-)present
     as d i f f u s e
and (loosely) effusive,
     voluminous b l o o m s
whose leafless lips (as opposed to those
who foliate, of course) confuse
     empathy and desire.

We are these enthusiasms.

The bruised music of our disillusion
     disinhibited
as a momentary anomaly coincides
with what might have been
     memory
in the Eternal recurrence of affinities
(or this would be ecstasy
dispossessed).

Let x = why,
not that this could be anything but
innate espousal.
The imaginary
as premonitory or, perhaps, rhapsody
's symptomatic caress.

Come dawn the stars / still
scintillate.

So Near, So Far

As the cold light of false promise fades
    a certain mania remains,
    mainly estrangement
       and flowery memory
without substance or reference,
    meaningless as
the specific gravity of anxiety
    yet essentially indicative,
if not exactly
    in the name of resonance,
    nonetheless inevitable
antidote to no known condition.

    No more
the correlation of these afflictions
    with those apprehensions,
or the state of being done, one
might say . . . an intimation
    of a like inclination
declines,
a flaw in feeling, perhaps
    amorous transference
to a mereness,
       or merely
    at a tangent to
useful delusion, not necessarily
without object or remedy.

A mode of dispassionate association,
     co-incident with distance,
reading the leaves of a clamorous present
     with the past attached
     to the eventuality
of unforeseen consequence.

In Differential Contingency

Now, broken among stones, to (dis-)
    locate / a way to endure
these isotopes of bodily sensation,
      to perturb the imperium
of sensoria, resonant with
      that very thing,
   chronicity.

       By the tyranny of
the numbers
and the implicit complacency
of cells,
     disturbed lands
  inhabited.

     At source
the inscrutable
chasm,
     concomitant rupture
in the flesh, inflammatory animus,
    thalamic anomalies
concatenated. Discordant

correspondence of psyche and symptom,
   whispering co-conspirators
   in metaphysical dissonance with
the sympathetic mysteries of
the interstitium.

Against circumstance,
a splintered equilibrium, intermittent
            r e s p i t e,
various antagonisms (dis-)
entangled / a way obscured,
        to illuminate the substrate
        or some lymphatic distillate
        of that somatic alembic
            instantiated.

As if distant
transmission, coded
signals echo,
        bone and hemogoblin,
autoimmune diffusion, systems
        nervous and nebular. Ob-
        durate spirit
persists, wounded and unwinding,
insistent resistance.

Interior Mirrors (Clearly Delirious)

I

Of radiance forthcoming,
    aura
incorporeal,
      glory ... body
           of luminosity
interanimates, becoming
null, exultant.

II

Opal hope enfolds
    the rose
of contradiction,
      sorrow's echo
           located ... so,
      antiphonal,
it goes.

Immanation: An Enclave

This that remains. Itself
    withheld. A certain species
        of feeling being
    shapely
        waves
    in configuration space.

    The thing (being)
acknowledged.

    The recognition of
a complex partial distortion,
or some form of contiguity
        disorder . . . intimate
        particulates glint
in elation . . . my own phonemes alone
        in the mycelial f e e l s.

Now everything.

Acknowledgements

Some of these poems previously appeared in *The Capilano Review*, *filling Station*, and *Touch the Donkey*, online at *The Alterran Poetry Assemblage* and *xStream*, and in the chapbooks *Time-Sensitive Material* (The Blasted Tree) and *Chronotope* (above/ground press).